PORTRAIT OF
HEREFORDSHIRE

Malcolm Scott

HALSGROVE

First published in Great Britain in 2007

Malcolm Scott
Aubretia Cottage,
Leigh
Worcestershire
WR6 5LA
Email: m.c.scott@post.harvard.edu
Phone: 01886 833526

British Library Cataloguing-in-Publication Data.
A CIP record for this title is available from the British Library.

ISBN 978 184114 644 7

HALSGROVE
Halsgrove House
Ryelands Industrial Estate
Bagley Road, Wellington
Somerset TA21 9PZ
Tel: 01823 653777
Fax: 01823 216796
email: sales@halsgrove.com
website: www.halsgrove.com

DEDICATION

Dedicated to my uncle, the late Gordon Scott, who
taught me about photography, art and seeing, and to
the new generation, my granddaughters Lucie Jane
Scott and Holly Dannemann-Scott and their brothers
Brian and Linus Denning.

Printed and bound in Great Britain by CPI Antony Rowe Ltd., Wiltshire

Foreword

by William Chase, founder of Tyrrells Potato Chips

This wonderful collection of contemporary photographs distinguishes itself from other published titles in its exclusive illustration of Herefordshire life in the twenty-first century. Yet, Malcolm Scott also beautifully alludes to memories and historic traditions which have passed into this millennium. It creates the comfortable juxtaposition of past and future, town and country, local and global, that makes Herefordshire such a charming place to live, work and enjoy.

The productivity of Herefordshire's people and its landscape has continued into this millennium. Our rich pastures produce natural ingredients for delicious local foods, from our apple orchards and potato fields, to resourceful rivers and family farms. Malcolm Scott affectionately draws attention to farming traditions all too familiar to me, as I have farmed Herefordshire land for 30 years.

His depiction of small scale manufacturers highlights the number and diversity of Herefordshire's talented and distinguished toymakers, basket makers, jewellers, artists, potters, farriers and silversmiths. They too are aware of the demand for locally produced, individual products. Herefordshire provides the perfect blend of gifted craftspeople, natural resources and inspiration to make both large and small scale businesses a valuable success.

However, it's not all about work. Herefordshire boasts a plethora of leisure activities. Our rivers, countryside and surrounding hills provide outstanding opportunities to hike, cycle, fish, canoe, shoot, horse ride and much more. So that the photographs of leisure activity in this book complete the Portrait of Herefordshire.

Contacts

Gregg's Pit Cider & Perry, Much Marcle, Herefordshire HR8 2NL **Phone:** 01531 660687 **Email:** info@greggs-pit.co.uk **Web:**www.greggs-pit.co.uk

Lyne Down Cider, Lyne Down Farm, Much Marcle Herefordshire HR8 2NT **Phone:** 07756 108501 **Email:** mark@lynedowncider.co.uk **Web:** www.lynedowncider.co.uk

Richard Vaughan, Pedigree Meats, Huntsham Farm, Goodrich, Herefordshire HR9 6JN **Phone:** 01600 890296 **Email:** Richard@Huntsham.com **Web:** www.Huntsham.com

Robin Clarke, Keepers House, Brockmanton, Leominster, Herefordshire HR6 OQU **Phone:** 01568 760272 **Email:** helenclarke52@tiscali.co.uk **Web:** www.robinschairs.co.uk

Sue Lane, 2 Fencote Station Cottage, Hatfield, Leominster, Herefordshire HR6 OSQ **Phone:** 01885 488836 **Email:** info@suelanejewellery.co.uk **Web:** www.suelanejewellery.co.uk

Bridget Drakeford, Upper Buckenhill Farmhouse, Fownhope, Hereford HR1 4PU **Phone:** 01432 860411 **Email:** bdrakeford@bdporcelain.co.uk **Web:** www.bdporcelain.co.uk

Caroline Hands, Overdine, Fownhope, Herefordshire HR1 4PT **Phone:** 01432 860402 **Email:**caroline.hands@talk21.com **Web:** www.archenfield.com/carolinehands.htm

Monkland Cheese Dairy, The Pleck, Monkland, Hereford HR6 9DB **Phone:** 01568 720 307 **Email:** enquiries@mousetrapcheese.co.uk **Web:** www.mousetrapcheese.co.uk

Acton Beauchamp Roses **Phone:** 01531 640433 **Email:** enquiries@actonbeaurose.co.uk **Web:** www.actonbeaurose.co.uk

Gabriel Pfeiffer, Frome Valley Toymakers, Unit 6, Hop Pocket Craft Centre, Bishops Frome, Hereford WR6 5BT **Phone:** 01885 490465 **Email:** gabrielpfeiffer@yahoo.co.uk **Web:** www.fromevalleytoymakers.co.uk

Jon Williams, Eastnor Pottery, Home Farm, Eastnor, Ledbury, Herefordshire HR8 1RD **Phone:** 01531 633886 **Email:** admin@eastnorpottery.co.uk **Web:** www.eastnorpottery.co.uk

Adam Watson, Faircraft, Clehonger, Hereford HR2 9SW (visits by appointment please) **Phone:** 0870 892 1814 **Web:** www.adamwatson.biz

Michael Burleigh, Horse Boutique, North Road, Kingsland, Leominster Hereford HR5 9SA **Phone:** 01568 708280 **Email:** enquiries@horseboutique.co.uk **Web:** www.horse-boutique.co.uk

Jeremy Atkinson, 44 Duke St, Kington, Herefordshire HR5 3DR. **Phone:** 01544 231683 **Email:** j@clogmaker.co.uk **Web:** www.clogmaker.co.uk

Christopher Lowder, Clemetis Cottage, Cradley, Malvern, Worcestershire WR13 5LQ **Phone:** 01886 880282

Peter Faulkner, 1 Clungunford Farmhouse, Clungunford Shropshire SY7 OPN

Dave Morris, Five Oaks, Eye Lane, Luston, Leominster Herefordshire HR6 ODS **Phone:** 01568 615711 **Web:** www.hfmg.org/producers/eye_game_larder.htm

Stephen Edwards, Four Poster Bed Company, New House Farm, Lyonshall, Kington, Herefordshire HR5 3JS, UK. **Phone:** 01544 340 444 **Email:** stephen@fourposterbed.co.uk **Web:** www.fourposterbed.co.uk

Jenny Crisp **Phone:** 01568 615772. **Email:** basket@ jennycrisp.co.uk **Web:** www.jennycrisp.co.uk

Will Chase, Tyrrell's Potato Chips, Tyrrells Court, Stretford Bridge, Leominster, Herefordshire HR6 9DQ **Phone:** 01568 720244 **Email:** info@tyrrellspotatochips.co.uk **Web:** www.tyrrellspotatochips.co.uk

Rob Lowe, Little Dunwood Farm, Weobley Marsh, Herefordshire HR4 8RR **Phone:** 01544 318 162 or 07970808489

Andrew James Marsden, Pittfield Farm, Pembridge, Leominster, Herefordshire HR6 9HY **Phone:** 07966163597 **Email:** marzypan8@hotmail.com

Ross Williams, The Wellington, Wellington, Herefordshire HR4 8AT **Phone:** 01432 830367 **Email:** info@wellington-pub. co.uk **Web:** www.wellingtonpub.co.uk

Andy Tobin **Email:** info@tobininstruments.co.uk **Web:** www.tobininstruments.co.uk

Tinsmiths, Tinsmiths Alley, 8A High Street, Ledbury, Herefordshire HR8 lDS **Phone:** 01531 632083 **Web:** www.tinsmiths.co.uk

Simon Vernon, The World's End Mapmaking Co Ltd., 134 Lots Road, London SW10 ORJ **Phone:** 020 7738 2206 **Email:** info@simonvernon.com **Web:** www.simonvernon.com

Introduction

However dedicated, most amateur photographers never have the opportunity to assemble a portfolio of related pictures large enough for an exhibition, let alone for a book. In this respect, I have been extraordinarily fortunate.

Back in 1970s I spent a year working in Pakistan, away from normal day-to-day responsibilities and with time to travel. This provided enough pictures for a one-man show at The Photographer's Gallery, London ("Pakistan: One Man's View"). And now, being virtually retired, I have been able to spend over three years producing enough photographs for this book.

The move to Herefordshire in 1974 was so that our children could have a country upbringing, and be part of a village community. The consequences of the move exceeded expectations, and I have been captivated by the county ever since. It is extremely rural, and very much all-of-a-piece. The only large town is Hereford, which is surrounded by five smaller market towns and then a host of villages, many of them very beautiful.

Although now it does not depend solely on agriculture for its wealth, Herefordshire certainly still depends on farming for its character, many of its leisure activities, and its varied landscapes. The county's scenery and its way of life have also made it a haven for one of the largest groups of artists and craftspeople in England.

The aim of this book is to try and portray this diversity, and to produce a composite portrait of Herefordshire. Although there are some landscapes and townscapes, the main focus has been on people at work and leisure. However, none of the pictures is "posed". For people at work, I simply watched what was going on before starting to take photographs, and then stayed long enough to try and do justice to the activity. This could take half a day, sometimes a day and, exceptionally, two days.

The whole project has been a rich and fascinating experience, and it only remains for me to thank those who have made it possible. Firstly there are those who have allowed me to photograph them at work. They are named in the captions, and their kindness, hospitality and patience added to the pleasure of watching them work. Then there are those who helped me to photograph a wide range of activities. They are Dominic Harbour and Val Hamer (Hereford Cathedral), Philip Blackman-Howard and Caroline Orgee (North Herefordshire Hunt), Will Chase, Paul Milton and Julie Lewis (Tyrrells Potato Chips), Yana Childs and Adrian Penning (Sun Valley), Donald Ree (Francis Willey), Richard Heatly (Herefordshire College of Art & Design), Rob Shiels (Special Metals Wiggin), Katie Phipps and Chris Jones (Bulmers), Leo Walsh (Wye Valley Chamber Festival), Tony Norman (The Leen, Pembridge), Mark & Betty Thompson-McCausland and the Oddsocks Theatre Company.

A very special thanks goes to Peter Wood, who took the door off his lovely two-seater plane so that I could have an unobstructed, if somewhat vertiginous, view of the countryside for the aerial photographs. In the process we learnt that using a GPS system had advantages over a road map. Thanks go to my wife, Lillian Somervaille, for her constant encouragement and invaluable criticism; and to her together with my younger daughter Kate and her partner Neil Leighton for acting as a selection committee. Finally it remains to thank Neil for editing and advising on the text and captions.

Malcolm Scott

Polytunnels near Leominster.

Dave Morris, game dealer, Luston.

After the harvest.

The Rector of Wigmore Abbey parish, Sylvia Turner, with one of her congregation at St Giles Church, Downton. The parish also covers the churches in Adforton, Brampton Bryan, Burrington, Elton, Leinthall Starkes, Leintwardine, Pipe Aston and Wigmore.

Graveyard at Ullingswick church.

Bookmakers at a Teme Valley Hunt Point-to-Point meeting, Brampton Bryan.

Teme Valley Hunt Point-to-Point, Brampton Bryan.

Spectators at the Teme Valley Hunt Point-to-Point horse races, Brampton Bryan.

Drapers Lane, Leominster.

Jenny Crisp, basket maker, Morton.

May Fair in Corn Square, Leominster.

Peter Faulkner, coracle and currach maker, Leintwardine.

The Herefordshire Beacon ("British Camp"), Malvern Hills.

Vet Roger Serres TB testing at Batchley Farm, Grendon Bishop.

Mary Jones, Batchley Farm, Grendon Bishop.

Batchley Farm yard, Grendon Bishop.

Along the Wye: Hoarwithy

Shooting party at Moor Court Farm, Stretton Grandison.

Pheasant shooting at Moor Court Farm, Stretton Grandison.

Peter Godsall with friends at a shoot, Moor Court Farm, Stretton Grandison.

Relaxing after a shoot in the old hop-pickers kitchen, Moor Court Farm, Stretton Grandison.

Traveller preparing parts for a new caravan along the A4103.

Christopher Lowder, freelance writer, journalist and editor, Cradley.

Vintage car display at Bromyard Gala.

Traction engine rally at Bromyard Gala.

Bromyard Gala fairground.

Miniature traction engine at Bromyard Gala.

Dispersal sale at Frome Manor Farm, Bishops Frome.

Young riders at a pre-hunt briefing of the North Herefordshire Hunt, Bredenbury.

North Herefordshire Hunt breakfast, Bredenbury

North Herefordshire Hunt meet, Bredenbury.

Edward Legge, retired farmer and part-time mole catcher, Stoke Lacy.

Large bale hauling.

Shaking down cider apples at Castle Farm, Yarkhill.

Grant Powell, agricultural contractor, unloading cider apples at Castle Farm, Yarkhill.

Ivor Hanson (left) and Donald Ree grading wool at Francis Willey, Bromyard.

Robin Clarke, chair maker, Brockmanton.

Charlie Postans, of Yew Tree Farm, Fromes Hill, shearing a Herdwick ram.

Ladies' Day at Hereford Races.

Simon Vernon, synoptic map maker (hand-drawn maps with architectural and topographical illustrations), Walford.

"Rappers" (sword dancers) rehearsing at the Bromyard Folk Festival.

Morris dancers outside the Hop Pole Hotel at the Bromyard Folk Festival.

Face painter at the Bromyard Folk Festival.

Brockhampton House, Brockhampton.

Gabriel Pfeiffer, toymaker, Frome Valley Toys, Bishops Frome.

St James church fete, Cradley.

Bric-a-brac stall, St James church fete, Cradley.

Frog racing at St James church fete, Cradley.

Lindsay Bousfield, grower of old roses, Acton Beauchamp.

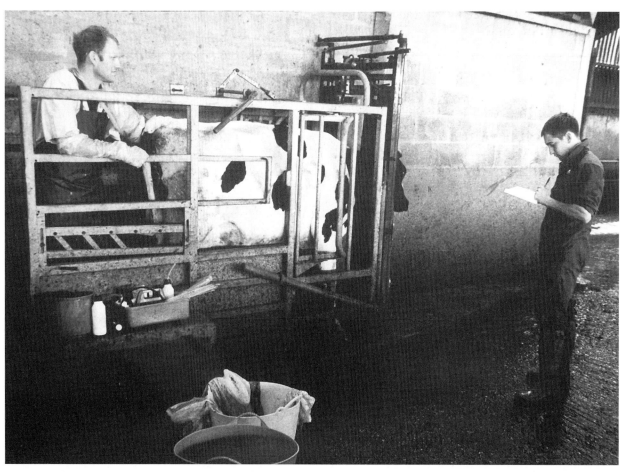

Vet Alistair Kenyon pregnancy testing a cow at Woofields Farm, Coddington, with the herdsman James Price.

Rosie Simcock in the herring-bone milking parlour of Woofields Farm, Coddington.

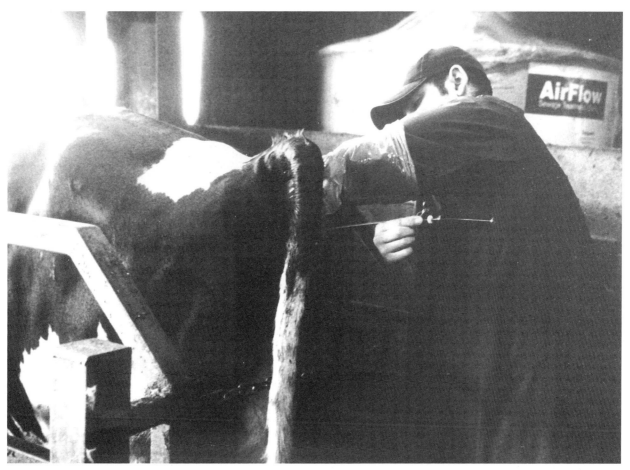

Andrew Baddeley (Genus ABS) artificially inseminating one of the 300 Holstein-Friesian cows at Woofields Farm, Coddington

Fred Simcock assisting a heifer to calve, Woofields Farm, Coddington.

Sue Lane, jeweller, Hatfield,

Garford Farm, Yarkhill, with the Malvern Hills in the distance.

Aidan Anderson, stone mason, working on one of the pinnacles of Hereford cathedral tower.

60

View towards the south-west from the top of the Hereford cathedral tower.

Nicola Kerridge, trainee stone mason, at Hereford cathedral.

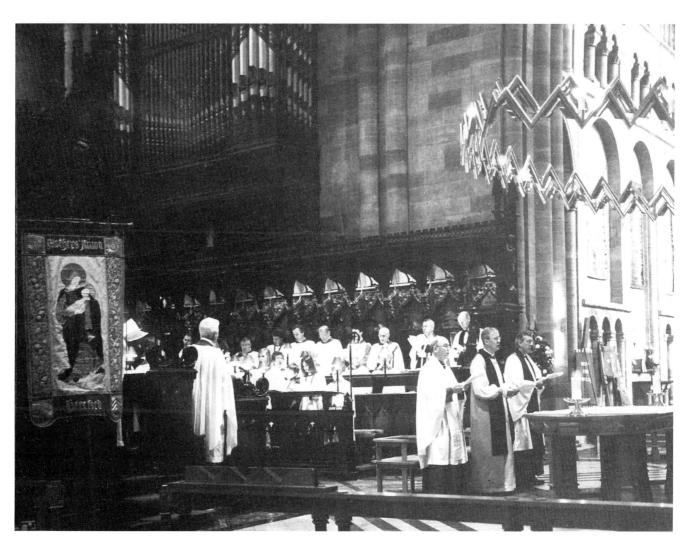

The Right Reverend The Lord Bishop of Hereford (centre) conducting the Mothers' Union Diocesan service in celebration of marriage.

Swimmers in the River Lugg at Lugg Bridge Mill, Hereford.

River Lugg in flood, Lugg Bridge Mill, Hereford.

The Left Bank, Hereford.

Lane to Hampton Wafre Farm, Docklow.

High Town, Hereford.

Wye Valley Chamber Music Festival: Tom Hankey (violin) , Joseph Tong (piano) & Amy Norrington (cello) rehearsing at the Bishop's Palace. Hereford.

69

David Probert (Sunderlands Sale Room) conducting a poultry auction at Hereford Market.

David Probert (Sunderlands Sale Room) conducting a poultry auction at Hereford Market; a customer is holding up the bird.

Hand-trimming chicken breast meat at Sun Valley. The foreground bin contains the trimmings. In the background, chicken legs are being de-boned.

Chickens entering the evisceration hall at Sun Valley, after being humanely slaughtered and then plucked.

Adam Watson, maker of books and bookbinder, Hereford.

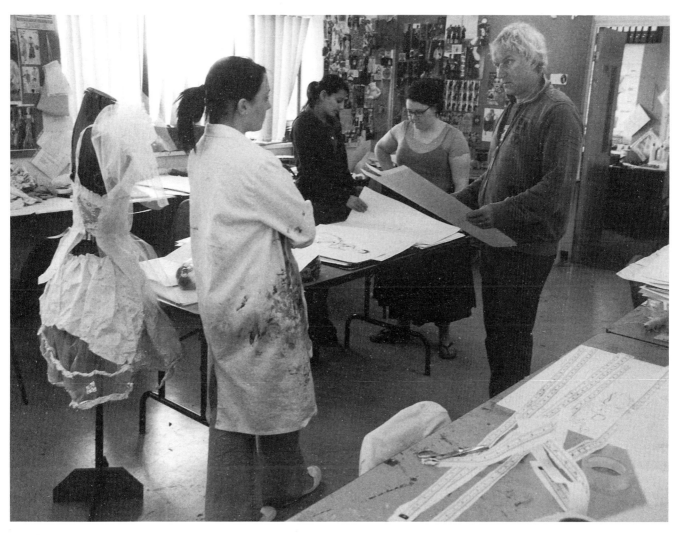

Mark Houghton, lecturer in National Diploma Art & Design at Herefordshire College of Art & Design, discussing projects with a 2nd year National Diploma textile student.

Group at a sheep auction, Hereford Market.

Casting nickel alloy ingots at Special Metals Wiggin, Hereford, one of Europe's leading nickel alloy specialists.

Potential buyers examining sheep at Hereford market.

Sheep pens at Hereford Market.

View of the fermentation vessels at Bulmers Cider, Hereford.

The cider fermentation process control room at Bulmers Cider, Hereford, with operators Dave Lea (left) and Mark Tracy.

Loading milled apples into a cider press, Lyne Down Farm, Much Marcle.

Sampling cider at Gregg's Pit, Much Marcle, during the Big Apple Festival.

Picking up cider apples at Gregg's Pit, Much Marcle.

Glass-bead maker, Diana Arseneau, at Pembridge Show.

Farmers' Market, Ross on Wye.

Ross on Wye.

The River Wye in flood at Ross on Wye.

Mothering pens at Haywood Farm, Callow.

Phil Dukes taking a ewe and her new-born triplets to a mothering pen at Haywood Farm, Callow.

Mervyn Thomas feeding new-born triplets at Haywood Farm, Callow.

First pasture for lambs at Merryhill Farm, Callow. The Malven Hills are in the background.

Viewing competition entries at the Herefordshire Young Farmers Club Rally, Elvastone Farm, Harewood End.

Women's tug-of-war at the Herefordshire Young Farmers Club Rally, Elvastone Farm, Harwood End.

Entertainment competition at the Herefordshire Young Farmers Club Rally, Elvastone Farm, Harewood End.

Morris dancers at Hellens, Much Marcle.

Horse ploughing at Wormside Agricultural Society's 161st Ploughing and Agricultural Competition, Bridge Farm, Kilpeck.

Ferguson TE20 tractor ("the little grey Fergie") ploughing competitions at the Wormside Agricultural Society's 161st Ploughing and Agricultural Competition, Bridge Farm, Kilpeck.

Parade of camelids at the 62nd Lea Residents Association Flower, Horse & Dog Show.

Start of a children's pony race at the 62nd Lea Residents Association Flower, Horse & Dog Show.

Billy Busker, traditional street entertainer, performing a levitation trick at the at the 62nd Lea Residents Association Flower, Horse & Dog Show.

Produce tent at the 62nd Lea Residents Association Flower, Horse & Dog Show.

View towards the Eastnor monument from the A449.

Bookies at the Radnor & West Hereford Hunt's Point-to-Point steeplechases, Cold Harbour, Monkland.

Bridget Drakeford, potter, Fownhope.

One of Fownhope Flower Club's 25th anniversary displays in aid of St Mary's church, Fownhope.

Rose Bennett training hop bines at Clastons Farm, Dormington.

Caroline Hands, artist, Fownhope.

Tall hops at Clastons Farm, Dormington.

Peter Davies, hop farmer, Clastons Farm, Dormington.

Trimming dwarf hops at Clastons Farm, Dormington.

Hop propogation at Clastons Farm, Dormington.

Rose Bennett with some of her family at Clastons Farm, Dormington.

Tying tall hops onto a conveyor for stripping at Clastons Farm, Dormington.

Percy Bennett with Rachel and Spider on their way into Herefordshire along the A4103.

Ben Bennett with chicken at Clastons Farm, Dormington.

Jon Williams, Eastnor Pottery.

Evening along the Wye: Strangford Farm, Sellack.

View east from the top of Hay Bluff, Black Mountains.

The Cat's Back and Black Hill, Olchon Valley.

At the Radnor & West Hereford Hunt's Point-to-Point meeting, Cold Harbour, Monkland.

Hunting supporter at the Radnor & West Hereford Hunt's Point-to-Point meeting, Cold Harbour, Monkland.

Spectators at the Radnor & West Hereford Hunt's Point-to-Point meeting, Cold Harbour, Monkland.

Matthew Allen, farrier's apprentice, making a shoe (plate) for a racehorse.

Vintage tractor display at the 62nd Lea Residents Association Flower, Horse & Dog Show.

Dodgems in Corn Square at the May Fair, Leominster.

Sampling newly pressed apple juice, Lyne Down Farm, Much Marcle, at the Big Apple Festival.

Poly-tunnels in winter, near Leominster.

South Hereford Hunt Harness Race at Home Farm, Allensmore.

Rob Lowe, master farrier, working at Walford.

Michael Burleigh, master saddle maker, Kingsland.

Weobley.

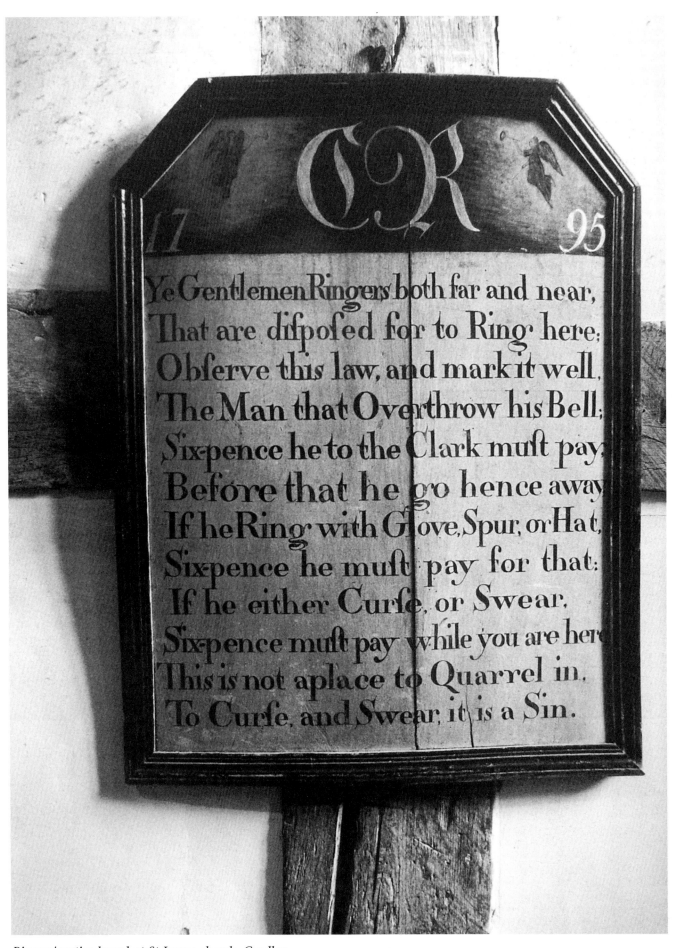

Ringers' notice board at St James church, Cradley.

Ringers' outing at the church of St Lawrence, Preston-on-Wye.

Kitchen garden at Hergest Croft.

Angela Conner's "Rocking Lady" at the "Sculpture in the Garden IV" exhibition at Hergest Croft.

Ledbury market hall.

Tinsmiths' show room, Ledbury.

Stephen Edwards, furniture maker, turning a bed post at the Four Poster Bed Company, Lyonshall.

James Roche and Thomas Francis, furniture makers, assembling a bed at the Four Poster Bed Company, Lyonshall.

Chip frying at Tyrrell's Potato Chips, Stretford Bridge.

Will Chase, founder of Tyrrells Potato Chips.

Harvesting potatoes for Tyrrells Potato Chips at Laddin Farm, Little Marcle.

Emma Harrington (foreground) and Sadie Hawkins making cheese at Monkland Cheese Dairy.

Along the Wye: Goodrich castle.

Richard Vaughan (Pedigree Meats) with some of his Middle White pigs. Huntsham Farm, Goodrich, has been in his family since 1650.

Eardisland.

Castle Weir House, Lyonshall.

Barbara Norman with her son Richard inspecting her herd of Hereford cattle at The Leen, Pembridge. Established in 1780, it is the oldest herd of Herefords in the world, and has been in her family since 1918.

Simeon Konsulov, a vet from Bulgaria, working in the rotary milking parlour at The Leen, Pembridge. In this, three hundred cows can be milked per hour.

Picnicing before the Oddsocks production of "The Taming of the Shrew" at Kinnersley Castle.

Oddsocks Production of "The Taming of the Shrew" at Kinnersley Castle.

Andrew James Marsden, silversmith, Pembridge.

Damson blossom along the A44 near Whitbourne.

Pembridge. The separate octagonal bell tower of St Marys church (top) is unique, and dates from the 13th century.

Jeremy Atkinson, master clog maker, Kington.

Andy Tobin, luthier (a maker of stringed instruments), Weobley Marsh.

Ross Williams at The Wellington public house & restaurant, Wellington (Flavours of Herefordshire "Pub of the year" in 2005 & 2006).

Sheep dog display at Dilwyn Village Show.

Trevor Hill, falconer, flying a young American bald eagle at the Dilwyn Village Show.

Children from Dilwyn Primary School maypole dancing at the Dilwyn Village Show.